PRAYER
THE IGNITED
POWER THAT BRINGS RESULTS

CELENA D. WILLIAMS

Uriel Press

Copyright © 2023 Celena D. Williams.

All rights reserved. No part of this book may be used or reproduced by any means, graphic, electronic, or mechanical, including photocopying, recording, taping or by any information storage retrieval system without the written permission of the author except in the case of brief quotations embodied in critical articles and reviews.

This book is a work of non-fiction. Unless otherwise noted, the author and the publisher make no explicit guarantees as to the accuracy of the information contained in this book and in some cases, names of people and places have been altered to protect their privacy.

Uriel Press books may be ordered through booksellers or by contacting:

Uriel Press
1663 Liberty Drive
Bloomington, IN 47403
www.urielpress.com
844-752-3114

Because of the dynamic nature of the Internet, any web addresses or links contained in this book may have changed since publication and may no longer be valid. The views expressed in this work are solely those of the author and do not necessarily reflect the views of the publisher, and the publisher hereby disclaims any responsibility for them.

Any people depicted in stock imagery provided by Getty Images are models, and such images are being used for illustrative purposes only.
Certain stock imagery © Getty Images.

Cover credit: Charlesia Howell and Marselina Williams

Scripture taken from the King James Version of the Bible.

ISBN: 979-8-8861-2026-4 (sc)
ISBN: 979-8-8861-2027-1 (e)

Library of Congress Control Number: 2023919855

Print information available on the last page.

Urial Press rev. date: 11/1/2023

To my children, Charlesia, Arthur, and Marselina. I thank the Lord for the three of you. While I raised you, we had some very difficult times, but the Lord never allowed any of you to be lacking. Remember what he did for you. I am the mom he blessed you with, but *he* is the Father who provided and protected you. He is the Father who will never disappoint or leave you. He is the Father who knows your value and your worth. Remember that.

We saw the power of prayer firsthand, when we were without a home and lived in a motel. On that blessed day, we each prayed, crying out to our Father for a home. Once we finished and opened our eyes, we saw the sun brightly beam as the rays pierced through open pockets in the clouds. We praised the Lord, because he heard our prayers and answered. Praise the Lord, he answered! Remember that.

Thank you for your support and encouragement. Most of all, thank you for celebrating with me after the last *t* was crossed and the last *i* was dotted. Yes, you all are grown and doing your own things, but remember how our Father invested in you. Give him a return on his investment. Love the Lord with all your hearts, and always seek him for guidance.

Love,
Mom

Contents

Acknowledgments ix
Introduction xi

1	Men Should Always Pray 1
2	Instant in Prayer 5
3	Pray without Ceasing 9
4	Praying Always.. 13
5	Come Boldly.. 17
6	Be Effective 21
7	Going Beyond the Ceiling 23

Prayer 27
Poem 29
About the Author 33

Acknowledgments

This book is one of many results that have taken place in my life due to the investments you have made in me. Yes, this is personal. I am the daughter of John Henry King Sr. He is best known by family and friends as Hen, but to me, he is Daddy. I love this man, and amazingly, he loves me. In my mind, I was his birthday present, since I was born on August 23, and his birthday is September 2. Daddy has always been a hard worker. As a little girl, I watched him work all day and study huge mechanical books at night. This man was dedicated to his studies and determined to reach his goal to work for the Railroad. I am proud to say he was a master mechanic until he retired.

Daddy, thank you for showing me the value of hard work. You played a key role in my existence here on earth. You spoke a blessing into my life when I was about twelve years old, and it has never left me. You said, "One day, you will be able to get your hair done every day if you want to." Now you come into my home every month and leave hairdo money. Daddy, it would take another book to say how much I love you. Look at the results of what the heavenly Father has allowed your little girl to accomplish in him. It will take me a lifetime to tell God how much I love and honor him. I am grateful for the special gift that he gave me. That gift is you, Daddy—a man I have loved all my life.

Pastor Vaughn Crawford, I will always be grateful to the Lord for you. What I am about to share is a clear picture of a skilled investor who did not know little eyes were watching when little ears could barely hear. My mom had a need. She was not a member of Dry Branch Church Of God In Christ, but my grandmother was. You had just become the pastor when she stated her need. I heard you say, "I don't have it with me, but come back, and I will give it to you." My little ears did not hear the request, and my little eyes did not see the exchange. But I saw the results of that exchange.

Pastor Crawford, I saw you take from your family and invest into mine. On that day, our Father knew I would remember the investment that you had made in me. He knew I would return and work diligently, serving in whatever way I could to show my appreciation for the man of God who planted a seed of giving for little eyes to see. Those same eyes have been trained and nurtured in the Word of God, under your leadership. I love and honor you, sir. Look at the return of your investment.

Carroll A. Walker, I will never understand why you're Mr. Carroll, but she's Mrs. Walker. I entered your life in 1995, when you placed an ad for a Housekeeper in the *Telegraph*. Out of all of the people interviewed, Mrs. Marianna Patton Ricketson Walker chose me. Now I know it was divinely ordered. Mr. Carroll, you and your wife provided an environment for me to experience a life completely different from the one I was accustomed to. You opened a new world for not just me but also for my children and, due to that, my grandchildren. You did not take a chance when you hired me. You invested in me.

Eventually, my duties changed from housekeeper to caregiver. I salute those who have the responsibility of caring for another. For me, it has been a privilege to serve you and your wife, Mr. Carroll. In 2021, my sweet and loving Mrs. Walker slipped into eternity at the age of 101. I loved that lady. I had the best job! We spent twelve hours a day together, and I spoiled her the entire time. After lunch, I was ordered to take a nap with Mrs. Walker, and needless to say, I obeyed. Thank you, sir. You gave me the freedom to care for her without any hesitation, because you knew I would do it with a spirit of excellence. The Lord knew what you needed before you placed the ad—just as he knew what I needed when I answered it. We needed each other. The Lord knew I would not leave her side until she entered into eternity. For twenty-six years, I served her, as I continue to serve you, Mr. Carroll. As a very successful businessman, you secured many prosperous investments, but the one you both made in me is priceless. Look at the result of your ad. You and your wife taught me how to serve and serve well. I will love you always, Mr. Carroll.

Dr. Roberta Andrews, through your loving hands I received a priceless gift. A powder and royal blue prayer shawl that belonged to your mother, Mrs. Allee Gardiner Hollis. I am grateful to you for not only caring for my physical needs but you invested into my prayer walk. Loving you forever.

Introduction

There have been many game shows where contestants have to choose a curtain, door, or box. Sometimes they choose the grand prize, such as the trip of a lifetime, a brand new car, or money. In all of these games, the contestants stand the chance of losing it all because they guessed wrong. As you read, you will discover that you are not in a game, but every time you participate in prayer, you enter a win-win situation. Prayer is a conversation with our Father who art in heaven. As Romans 8:26 says, Likewise the Spirit also helpeth our infirmities: for we know not what we should pray for as we ought: but the Spirit itself maketh intercession for us with groanings which cannot be uttered. Prayer support does not end there. We see Jesus on the right hand of the Father, interceding for us also. Romans 8:34

We have been granted permission to go behind the veil—a place that was once only accessible by priests. As a matter of fact, according to Matthew 27:50–51, the veil was torn from top to bottom when our great High Priest—who was nailed to the cross—yielded up the ghost. The invitation to come in and pray did not end there. As we see throughout scriptures, we are encouraged to seek his face and pray without ceasing. We do not have to be shy and fearful about it either. Hebrews 4:16 says, "Let us therefore come boldly unto the throne of grace, that we may obtain mercy, and find grace to help in a time of need."

Chapter 1

MEN SHOULD ALWAYS PRAY

> And he spake a parable unto them
> to this end, that men ought always
> to pray, and not to faint.
> —LUKE 18:1 (KJV)

There are times in our lives when we are caught off guard by situations or when circumstances stun us and leave us speechless. Being speechless is not always bad. Not every situation needs an immediate response. That brings to mind James 1:19, which says, "Wherefore, my beloved brethren, let every man be swift to hear, slow to speak, slow to wrath." We have to remember that when our lives seem to take a nosedive, our Father in heaven is not surprised by the current events. We may be beside ourselves, wringing hands and pacing the floor, or we may scratch our heads, wail, or remain completely speechless. Having a fortified prayer life will help us when we face challenges in this life. There are many examples in the Word of God. Let's take a look at Job. If he was interviewed on the evening news today, it would be something like this.

The studio commentator says, "Welcome to NCLC Live at five. Breaking News! Job, a local businessman in the land of Uz, tore up his clothes, shaved his head, and bowed on the ground. What possibly could have happened to cause this prominent member of society to publicly behave in this fashion?"

Sade Well, the reporter on the scene, says, "Wow, everything transpired so quickly. We were interviewing for the upcoming harvest festival hosted by the Men of the Gate Committee when the whole bottom fell out. Listen to this."

The one who got away steps in front of the camera and begins to tell his story. "Mr. Job's livestock—the oxen that were plowing and the asses that were feeding in the field—were stolen by the Sabean gang, who also killed the attending servants with the edge of the sword."

As the one who got away is speaking, another bearer of news walks up. "Mr. Job, the fire of God has fallen from heaven and burned up the sheep and servants, consuming them."

While he is speaking another bearer of news approaches and addresses Job. "The Chaldeans spotted three bands. They fell upon the camels and carried them away, slaying the servants with the edge of the sword in the process."

While he is speaking, another approaches. "Mr. Job, your sons and daughter were eating and drinking wine at their eldest brother's house when a great wind came from the wilderness. It smote the four corners of the house, which fell upon the young men and killed them."

Sade Well stares at Job, stunned. Nate, the cameraman, is so discombobulated that he's frozen. In his shock, the camera remains pointed at Job. This live feed is being broadcasted around the world. Viewers weep. Some are reminded of their lost businesses, homes, and loved ones. They're watching Job and his response to all this tragedy. What they see is shocking.

> Then Job arose, and rent his mantle, and shaved his head, and fell down upon the ground, and worshipped, And said, naked came I out of my mother's womb, and naked shall I return thither: the LORD gave, and the LORD hath taken away; blessed be the name of the LORD. (Job 1:20–21)

Job does not faint. He knows the vitality of being in constant communion with the Father, so he worships. How do we respond when we hear that something negative has happened to our homes, our cars, a long-anticipated trip, or an important event? We practically flip out. When Job experiences major loss, he worships. He does not know restoration is coming or that he will receive double. Job just does what is true to his nature and worships. Our prayer lives are so vital when things are going good. Having that strong connection prepares us for what is coming, so even though we may be shocked, our reaction is to worship. Job begins to pray for those who were supposed to be his comforting friends.

"In the midst of our sufferings and trials, we must remember there are others in more desperate situations than our own." Sade Well says. She and Nate wrap up their gear and head back to the studio.

At the studio, Nate is the first to talk. "In all my years spent covering tragic news stories, nothing—absolutely nothing has shaken me to the core like what I just witnessed. I remember the strong faith my grandfather had in the Lord and how devoted he was to prayer. What I just witnessed has reignited my trust in the Lord!" As the tears streamed down his face, he repented without shame or apologies.

Sade Well, with tears staining her face, praised the Lord! She had been praying for Nate continuously. Then today, which began like an ordinary day in the field, became a day of rejoicing. "I say unto you, that likewise joy shall be in heaven over one sinner that repenteth" (Luke 15:7).

The studio commentator says, "This has been NCLC Live at five. We're out!"

Chapter 2

INSTANT IN PRAYER

> Rejoicing in hope; patient in
> tribulation; continuing in prayer.
> —ROMANS 12:12 (KJV)

There are times in our walk when we desire something so strongly that we can see it manifest. These desires can be a spouse, children, money, a promotion, a home, or a car. But if it does not come when we want it, we become discouraged and withdrawn. We throw a huge pity party with a guest list that includes the famous party animals: Pink Pity, Rude Rock, Long Face Blue, and Sour Sand. As we all know, a good pity party is not complete until Trillionaire Twin Brother and Sister Misery show up. They are known to show up uninvited, because misery loves company. Their assignment is to talk about not only the present situation but also your past failures, mistakes, diet crashes, and bad relationships. These party crashers never come with anything positive or uplifting. They only spread gloom and doom.

The Word of God is so powerful! When these times come, we must remember that our strength and encouragement are within the holy pages of the Bible and in our hearts. During this process, we learn to trust God, because he knows what our desires will do to us if we obtain them too early. When we wait, we submit to his will for our lives. The first chapter of James is loaded with this powerful truth on patience, and in 1 Timothy

6:11, we are encouraged to follow patience. For some, *wait* is a bad word. People will pass you on a two-lane road with a hill, only to turn onto the next street.

Life situations can hit hard sometimes, and continuing to pray might not seem to make things better. But *prayer* is the only strength we have. Now is the time to dig in. The party animals and the twins don't have prayer lives. They have "talk about it" lives. They compete to find out who's the most miserable. They talk about who had the worst situation and then wallow in it. When you encourage yourself in the Lord, you remember how he moved the last time you waited for something, whether it was twenty years ago or an hour ago.

Praise the Lord! If we remember his faithfulness and what he has done, joy will flood our souls. Then we will quote his Word back to him and praise him with more intensity. As the praises flow, we will sense his presence. Our tears will feel like hot lava streaming down our cheeks. It will be as if we have ten thousand tongues that move simultaneously. We will praise him until we find ourselves on our knees, bowed down as low as we can go. Worship for the almighty God will explode from the very core of our beings! And then we will pray.

I married at the age of twenty-three. I'm saved and enjoying my new life with the Lord now, but about five years in, married life was hard and getting harder. I loved my husband, but he did not love or want me. The stress of knowing this got to me. One day, on the way home from work, I stopped at my church. I did not have a key to get in, but just being on the grounds brought peace and calm to my spirit. The tears flowed and flowed. I couldn't stay in the car, so I went to the backside of the church, behind the kitchen. It became that sacred place, as described in Psalm 91:1. Kneeling down on the ground, the church became my altar. I prayed, for it was all I knew to do. I don't remember the prayer, but the Lord does. Humbling before him while knowing he was the only one who could help me caused the floodgates to open. I was wrapped in the arms of the Lord. Eventually, the marriage ended, *but* my connection to the Lord was solid. I dug in, because I had three children to raise. I did not have room to flip or pass out.

The Word of God is our anchor in the middle of life's storms. "Casting all your care upon him; for he careth for you" (1 Peter 5:7). The amazing gift of prayer reminds us of his love toward us, his children. He always has time for us. He knows what we are going to say before we say it. "Praise God, he already has the answer" (Isaiah 65:24). Whatever the situation, keep praying. We will go to the extreme to get something that will bring pleasure for a moment, so we must go to the extreme to maintain our relationship with the Lord. When things happen, prayer must be instant.

Chapter 3

PRAY WITHOUT CEASING

> Pray without ceasing.
> —1 THESSALONIANS 5:17 (KJV)

First Thessalonians 5:17 is vital to our prayer lives. We can't be a "hit it and quit it" generation when it comes to prayer. When a need comes to our attention, we must take hold of it, until the manifestation materializes. How many times have we stopped praying about something because we did not see immediate results or were discouraged? You knew that prayer sailed all the way to the Lord. It was one of those prayers where every word was precise. Your tone was on point, and you bowed just so. There was no mistake about it. When you opened your eyes, you knew that the prayer would manifest, but then nothing happened. You kept at it for a few more days, before discouragement finally set in. Doubt overtook your faith, and your prayer ceased. But this is a new day! Praying without ceasing is action.

SITUATIONS

PIPE

MW and his wife noticed a faint smell of mildew in their home. They could not find the source of the odor, so they soon dismissed it. As time moved on, the smell got stronger and stronger. Finally, they couldn't take it any longer and called in an expert to locate the source of the odor. The expert revealed the problem. Their water pipe had a pin-sized hole that was leaking, causing water to seep into the foundation. All that damp moisture in the basement caused mold and mildew to grow. The condition was so bad that the couple will have to move out immediately. The undetected pinhole caused significant damage to the home. What would happen if we prayed the way that the water dripped out of the pipe? What kind of damage would we do?

> So shall they fear the name of the LORD from the west, and his glory from the rising of the sun. When the enemy shall come in like a flood, the Spirit of the LORD shall lift up a standard against him. (Isaiah 59:19)

FAUCET

There is nothing more irritating than a dripping faucet. You try everything possible to fix it to no avail. Adjusting the knobs worked temporarily. Then *drip, drip, drip, drip*. Eventually, you decide to buy a new faucet. "A continual dropping in a rainy day and a contentious woman are alike" (Proverbs 27:15). Merriam-Webster defines *contentious* as "exhibiting an often perverse and wearisome tendency to quarrels and disputes." What would happen if we took on the dripping faucet method with our prayers? When we pray about something without ceasing, change will come. So we can't let up. We must plow through and stay focused. After a while, victory will come.

BOXING

A person uneducated in boxing terms would not fully understand what goes on in the ring. They would only see someone get knocked down, allowing the other person to win. But there are two ways to knockout an opponent: technical knockout (TKO) and knockout (KO). According to Merriam-Webster, a TKO is "the termination of a boxing match when the boxer is unable or is declared by the referee to be unable (because of injuries) to continue the fight." A KO is "to defeat (a boxing opponent) by a knockout" according to Merriam-Webster. This means the person is unconscious, like David knocked out Goliath in 1 Samuel 17: 1–54.

As children of God, we cannot walk in defeat, not when Romans 8: 37 declares, "Nay, in all these things we are more than conquerors through him that loved us." Praying without ceasing empowers us to not only stand up to the Goliaths in our lives but also run to them, declaring the Word of God. We know his Word will guide us right to the spot where our Goliaths will come down, not by a TKO but by KO.

I also want to discuss the southpaw stance. According to dictionary.com, southpaw is "a boxer who leads with the right hand and stands with the right foot forward, using the left hand for the most powerful blows." The power is in the left hand, surprising the opponent.

> For the Word of God is quick, and powerful, and sharper than any two edged sword, piercing even to the dividing asunder of soul and spirit, and of the joints and morrow, and is a discerner of the thoughts and intents of the heart. (Hebrews 4:12)

What would happen if a situation came where we led with our right hand, which was prayer, and hooked with our left hand, the Word of God? That is where the power is! Our opponent will be defeated. Studying is vital to a child of God, because the Bible is loaded with sixty-six books full of firepower. The Word of God coupled with unceasing prayer are the only weapons we will ever need. They will bring the work of the enemy down. Pray without ceasing.

Chapter 4

PRAYING ALWAYS

> Finally, my brethren, be strong in the
> Lord, and in the power of his might.
> —EPHESIANS 6:10

The strength and power mentioned in Ephesians 6:10–18 is of the Lord. He permits us to obtain and use these attributes to fortify ourselves in the spirit. Helping my children prepare for prom was an experience. There had to be color coordination between them and their dates. What's amazing about this is the amount of time it took to select a color. With all the choices that are available, a parent can get dizzy just looking at color swatches. Once the color was selected, we began the painstaking work of finding the right dress and all of its accessories: shoes, jewelry, and makeup. We also needed to worry about how the hair, nails, and toes would be done. The tux needed a vest, cummerbund, cufflinks, suspenders, socks, and shoes. He needed a haircut as well. And they needed a ride!

All of this preparation was done for an event that lasted about four hours. Every single penny spent was unrecoverable. The tux and accessories went back to the rental facility. The dress—which was found after visiting five stores and cost what some parents would have paid for a night at a very exclusive hotel and dinner at a five-star restaurant—was balled up on the closet floor. The shoes hurt her feet, so she only wore them long enough to take pictures.

You may ask what prom preparations have to do with Ephesians 6:10-18. We put so much time, money, and effort into things that only last a moment. Don't misunderstand me. It's good to support our children and allow them to experience their special events, but we must teach them how to fight spiritual battles. These battles are the main events that will come into their lives long after prom is over, and the attire cannot be purchased from a rack, rented, or ordered from a catalog. This attire—the armour of God—has been tailor-made in heaven. It was designed exclusively for the "heirs of God, and joint-heirs with Christ" (Romans 8:17). This armour equips us to stand against, wrestle with, and withstand our opponents. Praise God!

Ephesians 6:11–12 gives a clear picture of what we wrestle with. The only way we can win the match is by using our God-given weapons. My son, Arthur, attended Tattnall Square Academy, where he became interested in the wrestling program. He did very well during practice and the few meets that were held. His weight class was 218. One day, my schedule allowed me to attend his match for the first time. Big mistake. There's such a thing as moms' wrestling etiquette. From what I could understand, Arthur was doing well, but then he was pinned down. To me, all he needed to do to get out of the hold was flip the guy. I ran down the bleachers, trying to make eye contact with my son. No one told me to stay put, and I thought that if I yelled louder than everyone else in the crowd, my son would flip his opponent and win the match. However, once we made eye contact, I realized I wasn't giving him support. I was being a major distraction. He lost the match, and I learned that the best way to help was to sit still and yell. He could close his eyes and hear me over all the other voices, not distracting him but encouraging and supporting. Arthur did not quit. He continued and won the state championship in his weight class for two years in a row—the first person to do so in Tattnall's history.

We must understand the armour is not just for us. According Ephesians 6:18, the saints are included. We are our brothers' keepers. We must stay focused, because distractions will try to throw us off track. Perseverance is in our arsenal, always ready. Being diligent in securing every area of our armour fortifies us in the spirit so "that ye may be able to withstand in the evil day" (Ephesians 6:13). We have to be able to stand! Ask yourself the following. What connects all this together? What completes the outfit?

What is the most vital aspect? What must take place when the armour is completely in its respective place? The answer is prayer!

> Take unto you the Whole Armour of God: Stand therefore, having your loins girt about with truth, and having on the breastplate of righteousness; And your feet shod with the preparation of the gospel of peace; Above all, taking the shield of faith, wherewith ye shall be able to quench all the fiery darts of the wicked. And take the helmet of salvation, and the sword of the Spirit, which is the word of God. Praying always with all prayer and supplication in the Spirit, and watching thereunto with all perseverance and supplication for all saints. (Ephesians 6:18).

Chapter 5

COME BOLDLY

> Let us therefore come boldly unto the
> throne of grace that we may obtain mercy,
> and find grace to help in time of need.
> —HEBREWS 4:12

Before we come boldly, we must understand the power and intimacy of the foundation that we kneel on. This foundation is the Word of God. How Hebrews 4:12 describes the action of the Word is a clear picture of the power and deepness that we possess as believers in Christ. The Word goes where no human-made device can ever go. The Word penetrates to the very core of whatever we apply Him to. Yes, Him. "IN the beginning was the Word, and the Word was with God, and the Word was God" (St. John 1:1). "And the Word was made flesh, and dwelt among us, (and we beheld his glory, the glory as of the only begotten of the Father,) full of grace and truth" (St. John 1:14). That is the power of his Word!

Please read chapters 1 and 2 of Genesis. God said, "Let there be," and it was and still is. Think about the power of his Word. Everything God spoke continues in its place. The sun, moon, stars, oceans, fowl, fish, and earth are all due to the power of his Word. As his children, we can utilize the gift that he has given to us. Throughout the Bible, we see countless acts of boldness. The one that first comes to mind is David and Goliath.

In 1 Samuel 17:1–58, a youth with a sling and stone went against a giant with a sword, spear, and shield. It was a battle of epic proportions. David came in the name of the Lord. The stone took the giant down, and David, with his bold self, took the giant's head.

Hebrews 4:12–16 encourages us believers to see the gift that we have been given. We can enter this sacred place—the presence of the Creator of the heavens and earth. God "breathed into the nostrils of man the breath of life; and man became a living soul" (Genesis 2:7). We can come into his presence! Hold onto that thought. Some of you just went into praise. Someone just took a breath and said, "Praise the Lord." Someone just threw their hands in the air and shouted, "Hallelujah!" Go on and praise him.

A perfect picture of boldness that we may have overlooked is told in St. Matthew 15:21–28 and St. Mark 7:24–30. The Syrophenician woman is Greek, not a Jew. Her young daughter has an unclean spirit, so she goes to Jesus on her daughter's behalf. Once this mother heard about Jesus, she did not allow her nationality, her financial status, the disapproving disciples, or Jesus's comment to stop her. She was at the throne of grace, and she fell at his feet, asking him to have mercy on her. She called him "Lord." She knew how to act and how to ask. That is bold!

Throughout the New Testament, we constantly see parents go to Jesus for their children. Look at the power of this realization. We must bring our children to the Lord! They may be grown and gone, but that does not give us an excuse not to pray for them. When we are in God's presence, staying focused is vital. When the crumbs fall, you will know where they will land. "Praise be to God" (Psalm 107:8). "We have seats at the table! Therefore we can come boldly unto the throne of grace. Her petition was granted. She had the green light" (Romans 2:10–11).

There are times when we must get low in order to look up. Praise the LORD! As Romans 10:15 says, when we're low, we can see God's feet. When we see the feet, we know good news is coming. There is never a time to quit. We must be like Jacob in Genesis 45:16–28, when he saw the wagons rolling in. The provisions were a blessing, but even better was knowing that his son Joseph, who he was told died, was actually alive.

Joseph was not only alive but also large and in charge, sending wagons in the middle of a famine. Who does that? Our Father. Do you have a famine in your life right now? Whether you suffer from a great shortage, lack, or deficiency, come boldly to our Father!

Chapter 6

BE EFFECTIVE

> The effectual fervent prayer of a righteous man availeth much.
>
> —JAMES 5:16

My mom, Betty Jean King, was one of those ladies who was small in stature but could out talk and out fuss anyone. Those who knew her would say, "Amen." Not long after I cried out to the Lord to save me, she became ill. The diagnosis was lung cancer. But my mom wasn't afraid of anything. If the fan or electric heater cord blew up, she would cut the bad part off, splice it, add a new cord with black electrical tape, and plug it back in. If she spliced and taped electronics in my presence, I was out the door and ready to call 911. If I was in a rocking chair at the time, all you would see is a chair empty of its occupant. I ran from electricity alterations but not Betty Jean. She was also known for her laugh—a trait all six of her children inherited. One night, we laughed so hard that Grandma Marzie screamed at us to shut up. She said, "All of y'all need to be in a grinning school." We received a lot of medicine that night, for "a merry heart doeth good like a medicine" (Proverbs 17:22 KJV).

If your parents or loved ones are in need of care, don't leave the responsibility to one or two relatives. This is a time for all hands to be on deck. Please let go of what you didn't get as a child. Forgive them for your sake. Yes, it hurts and is painful, but please forgive so that you can heal.

As Mom's health declined, my siblings did an amazing job caring for her. I filled in when I could. I remember one night, while she was in the ICU. The waiting room was full of people ready for the next visiting hour. Like so many others who were there for the night, I had the necessary supplies: my Bible, food, drink, phone, books, pillow, and blanket. At a certain point, I became restless, so I went down to the chapel. When I entered, it was empty. I kneeled down at the altar and prayed. Some might consider it small prayer, but it had tremendous results. Part of the prayer was for her to be spared so that I could be a better daughter.

When I finished praying, I rose to leave. In the back of the chapel, near the exit, was a big Bible. It was completely closed and looked brand new. When I opened it, it opened to Luke 11:9–10: "And I say unto you, Ask, and it shall be given you; seek, and ye shall find; knock, and it shall be opened unto you. For every one that asketh receiveth; and he that seeketh findeth; and to him that knocketh it shall be opened." Praise the Lord! He heard and answered my prayer. Our mom and a gentleman were the only two who came out of the ICU. If our mom had died that night, I wouldn't have had the opportunity to lead her to Christ. She accepted the saving grace of the Lord.

I'm sure many of you have had events in your, when your prayers were effective. The size of the prayer doesn't matter. It only matters that we prayed. "Confess your faults one to another, and pray one for another, that ye may be healed. The effectual fervent prayer of a righteous man availeth much" (James 5:16 KJV). To give you a biblical example, look at 1 Samuel 30:1–31. The situation is explained in verses 1–6. The action takes place in verse 7. David prays in verse 8, and the Lord answers him. In verses 9 and 10, David shows his obedience. Provision are made in verses 11–17. David's prayers are answered in verses 19 and 20. Finally, victory and praise are achieved in verses 21–31. All of this was possible because David was effective!

Chapter 7

GOING BEYOND THE CEILING

> And when he had taken the book, the four beasts and four and twenty elders fell down before the Lamb, having every one of them harps, and golden vials full of odours, which are the prayers of saints.
> —REVELATION 5:8

I've been a member of New Community Life Church for about twenty-four years. My pastor, Vaughn Crawford, has a skill that I have tried repeatedly to master but have not successfully obtained. That skill is the way he wraps an extension cord. I know some of you asked, "A what?" Yes, an extension cord. See, this skill is simple but powerful. When he has finished using the cord, it is wrapped neatly and hung up or placed in the toolbox. The way he wraps the extension cord causes everything to be precise. Neither the size nor the length matters, because he will wrap it precisely each time. This shows persistence, commitment, and dedication to doing things with a spirit of excellence.

What does an extension cord have to do with prayer? The key component needed to receive what you seek is faith-filled prayer. To cause our prayers to go beyond the ceiling, we cannot be sloppy when we go before the Lord of all creation. Praying out of habit without the foundation of the Word, faith, hope, or expectation will not reach the light bulb, let alone go beyond the ceiling.

The story of David in 1 Samuel 30:1–31 is one of my favorites to read. It's filled with shock, suspense, drama, murder, and charity. King David was known for being a man after God's heart. He was a man of praise and worship. No one could out praise David! When they brought the ark of God back into the city, David and the entire house of Israel shouted and sounded the trumpet. David leapt and danced before the LORD (2 Samuel 6:16). He had no shame in giving the LORD what was due to him. His relationship with the LORD was vital to his survival, not just as a king but also as a husband and father. For David, going into the presence of the LORD and just flopping down was not an option.

In 1 Samuel 30:6–8, David and his men return home to Ziglag, only to find it burned down and the women and children missing. Imagine how they must have felt. They'd anticipated the reception they would receive upon entering the city. The elders were supposed to greet them at the gate with cheers, music, and dancing from the townsfolk. Children should have run alongside them, excited to see the men of valor return from battle with their spoils. David and his men had long awaited the embraces of their wives, home-cooked meals, and hot baths. But Ziglag was destroyed. They were in shock. One day as a child, I was playing down the hill and couldn't hear my mom call for me. She whipped me so badly that I was still trying to catch my breath after it was over. It was like my chest was trying to catch up to my heart. The rest of me just passed out. "Three switches plaited together were used very well that day." That was the first time I knew how David and his men felt. "Then David and the people that were with him lifted up their voice and wept, until they had no more power to weep" (1 Samuel 30:4). But in the midst of it all, God had a plan.

Even though all of them were in the same situation, David's men wanted to stone David because he was the leader. When people are hurting, they tend to lash out at the ones closest to them. For example, children who are hurt or disappointed by one parent sometimes take their frustrations out on the parent who is working nonstop to take care of them. But David's response was so powerful. He didn't just flop down and uttered a pity-filled prayer. He encouraged himself in the LORD! According to Merriam-Webster's Dictionary, *encourage* means to give help or to inspire.

I believe David remembered how the LORD delivered him from the bear, the lion, and Goliath. More importantly, David remembered the LORD's power and how the LORD caused words and songs to pour out of him. Praise the LORD! David encouraged himself and then prayed, because he knew how to approach God. He knew how to get results.

Take a closer look at David, not the king or man of worship but the man of war who had skilled men alongside him. They could have tracked down the Amalekites and done their best to beat them down. But what would they have lost? A lack of prayer affects everyone, just as continual prayer affects everyone. So who was involved? David; his six hundred men; their wives and children; the townspeople; Abiathar the priest, the Egyptian, who spent three days laying in a field; the elders of Judah; David's friends; the people in Bethel, South Ramoth, Jattir, Aroer, Siphmoth, Eshtemoa, Rachal, Jerahmeelites, Kenites, Hormah, Chorashan, Athach, Hebron, and all the other places that David and his men went to. Look at everyone who would have missed out if David had not prayed. He would have been running on emotions and his own ability, making him ill prepared. Being ill prepared for war is dangerous because then we move with only our own strength.

Pity doesn't move God. It only intensifies the pity you already have for yourself. Encourage yourself and remember what the LORD has done. This current thing did not take him by surprise. Pray fervently, as David did, and see how it affects everyone involved. My pastor would pray, and if you were attentive, you would know when he had entered the throne room. You could hear it and be drawn in. As members, we should know our shepherd's voice and be drawn in. Then, as he prays, we will pray. When he says, "Yes, LORD," we will say, "Yes, LORD." If he says, "Praise the LORD," so will we. We should be in unison when it comes to the Spirit. Then, the next thing you know, someone is being blessed. That person feels the presence of the LORD. They are being touched and encouraged. If we are connected, we all go beyond the ceiling.

Think about your location of prayer. It could be your church, home, office, or car. The time of day doesn't matter, so long as you are in prayer. That prayer will travel from the depths of you, through your esophagus, and out your lips. It will go past the light bulb and through the ceiling, to where you have already gone beyond the troposphere—into the stratosphere.

This is when distractions will try to hinder your spiritual travel, so you must remain persistent. Spiritually fly high, like a commercial jet. "Holy Ghost Airline" Your prayer will move at a speed that humans cannot clock as it goes to the mesosphere. This sphere extends above the planets. Most meteors burn up in this sphere, but your prayer should intensify. Let the Word of God flow out of you while your prayer continues moving. The fervent heat of the atmosphere will cause praise to come forth. At the same time, your prayer language will change. It will become unknown when your prayer reaches the thermosphere, where auroras occur, causing beautiful displays. The temperatures can reach up to five hundred degrees Fahrenheit, but that heat is nothing compared to a saint of God who is on fire in the Holy Ghost. And the displays do not compare to one who knows Psalm 119:105: "Thy word is a lamp unto my feet and a light unto my path."

If you keep praying, you will enter the last frontier exosphere, where the air is extremely thin. Don't quit, because you're praying to God, the one who breathed into the nostrils of man, and he became a living soul. He also breathed and said, "Receive ye the Holy Ghost." This sphere should not intimidate you. It should remind you of the power of God, the Creator of the heavens and the earth. If you remain dedicated, you will go beyond the ionosphere. That sphere is halfway to the moon, but you will go beyond it to enter a place that I call the prayernado zone. Because of your persistence, commitment, and dedication to pray, a firestorm from the Spirit will be set off. Enter into his gates with thanksgiving, and into his courts with praise: be thankful unto him, and bless his name. (Psalm 100:4). You will boldly enter the throne of grace! Once there, you can ask for what you want, because God will have drawn you to him at that very hour. He will want to hear your voice say what he put in you to say to him. No one can say it like you.

Yes, pray! As you do so, you're in his presence. Situations will change, and restoration will take place. When you enter in you have gone beyond the ceiling, through every sphere known to man, and into the throne of God. Let's ignite the power!

Prayer

Heavenly Father, thank you for this finished work. As my brothers and sisters dig deeper and cultivate their prayer lives may the power of your presence radiate through them. When situations arise may their first response be prayer. May they remember when the storms of life kick up, your Word is the anchor that holds them steady. Understanding that, your Word coupled with praise and past victories, the storm on the inside of them is raging greater than what is kicking up outside. With the fruit of their lips, a Prayernado has let loose in the spirit. Fill them the more with your anointing that yokes are destroyed. In Jesus Name, Amen

Poem

Painting by Sydney Sams

Let everything that hath breath praise
the LORD. Praise ye the LORD.
— PSALM 150:6

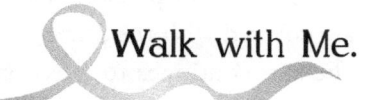
Walk with Me.

Time is set forward because spring has sprung. The morning dew is no longer stiff and icy but glistening by the warmth of the new season.
As we close the door behind us, the aroma of new blooms of roses captivates our senses and causes a smile to take over our features. We realize we are truly alive and breathing.
Praise ye, the LORD.

The beauty of the day surrounds us, and a hum begins to rise up from within, with each step we take. The anticipation of what lies ahead causes our hearts to race as we quicken our pace—as the aromas of every blooming flower are awakened to full strength and beauty.
Praise ye, the LORD.

Coming to the clearing of the luscious path, our eyes and the very core of our being are in awe of what is before us. See it for yourself.

The path opens up to the most beautiful valley ever seen by the human eye. As we step out, we behold the greenest, most well-manicured grass ever seen—thick and beautiful. We can hear frogs croaking, crickets chirping, birds singing, and squirrels racing from tree to tree.

The creek flows easily, as it navigates the edge of the bank and the rocks within. Look there: a school of fish jumping and diving in the flow.
As our gazes turn upward, we are floored by what we see. As the sun rises, a gentle breeze causes the leaves to sway, as if they were participating in a dance to a lovely song played skillfully by an unseen orchestra.

The hum within us matches the sway and the sounds around us. Off in the distance, we see an eagle rise higher and higher with the gentle breeze. As he soars, his wings expand to their full length. Our hum is intensifying!

Then there are mountains so massive that they look like they were carved by a master sculptor. Their form was cut precisely to match the creation of the valley. Their peaks are covered with the purest snow, which can be seen from a distance. As the sun continues to rise, something amazing happens. The mountain awakens!

As the eagle crests the peaks with its wings expanded, the frogs, crickets, squirrels, fish, creek, wind, leaves, blooming flowers, us, and the snow-capped mountains awaken, with vapors rising up. The hum from us all explodes in one voice!

Praise the LORD! Praise the LORD! Praise the LORD! Praise the LORD! As we praise him, the mountain begins to quake. The earth shakes. The creek stills. The aroma around us is so intoxicating that we are on our faces on the valley floor, completely prostrated. Only our mouths are moving, exalting him and praising him. It is not fear that has captivated us but reverence. We are in the presence of our King, our LORD, our Savior, our Protector, our Healer, our Love. His presence has inhabited us!

Praise ye, the LORD.

About the Author

Celena Williams is a licensed Evangelist and member of New Community Life Church in Dry Branch, Georgia. She serves as Chaplain with the Twiggs County Sheriff's Office. Also, is a past President of the Pilot Club of Macon. She is the Owner of Fruit of Her Hands Treasures and Gift Shop in Jefferesonville, Georgia and Has been a Private Caregiver for 27 years and counting.

She is a blessed mother of three; Charlesia (Melvin) Howell, Arthur Williams, Marselina Williams.

To her Howell grandchildren she is affectionally know as HoneyGram; Markia, Makenzi, Nathan, Natalie(at rest) Machelle and Nehemiah

www.ingramcontent.com/pod-product-compliance
Lightning Source LLC
LaVergne TN
LVHW091321080426
835510LV00007B/592